Life Reflections

Sara Ureel

Printed in the United States of America
ISBN: 978-1-956019-72-8 (paperback)
ISBN: 978-1-956019-73-5 (ebook)

**Canoe Tree
Press**

4697 Main Street
Manchester Center, VT 05255
Canoe Tree Press is a division of DartFrog Books

Contents

I dedicate this book to God, who placed these words in my heart;
to my husband, Emil, who loves me for who I am and saw the poet within;
to Sherri, who remains undoubtedly my cheerleader throughout;
to Nadine, who enjoyed our poetry readings;
and to Joy, who always lent a listening ear to the creative process.

A journey I never had planned to take but have
been blessed as I stepped out in faith.

Moments In Time

Cleansing Rain

Trees, flowers, grass,
The spring rain is welcomed
By the creation of our world

People scurry
Shelters are temporarily found
With a canopy of jackets sighted overhead

The animals too, find their resthaven
In the saturated scenery, I stand there
My clothes drenched

The downpour of rain
Quenches the thirst of nature's dry ground
Like the heavens opened up and turned on a hose
Where everything's a blurred watercolor

Chilled to the bone
My thoughts seem to disappear
Rolling down my back to the tips of my toes

Similar to the rain
Purifying the earth
God makes our cluttered minds clear
He takes our worries and fears
He vanquishes our hurts and pain
So we can smile and dance in the rain

Those Sweet Summer Nights

Listening to the campfire crackle and pop
I slump back in my chair, holding my mug
Reminiscing on the day we had
The children's pent-up excitement
Makes the cool night air warmer
With marshmallows still stuck on their faces
They finally fall asleep
Dreaming sweet dreams
Those summer nights
The world seems to take a pause
The smells of campfires linger in the air
As the glow fades
The embers dim
Oh, those sweet summer nights

Nothing Ever Happens

Nothing ever happens in my yard until I see
Nests made with such love
Ants busy at work, moving dirt from one place to the next
Spiders flying in the air to attach their web

Nothing ever happens at home until I see
My children grab a ball to play soccer
When we sit together and enjoy a home-cooked meal
When I see excitement in our children's eyes retelling their day

Nothing ever happens in my spiritual walk until I see
That listening to Jesus needs quiet reflection
When insignificant requests get answered
When a song touches my heart and I know who put it there

When God surrounds me wherever I walk
When I think nothing is happening
My eyes are opened to see
Life in the nothings of our days

Walking in Wonder

Walking in wonder
Children's eyes roam
Taking in everything they pass
A fascination on their faces
That remains intense
Their little hands touch everything in sight

Taking a deep breath
They breathe in life around them
Children see with their hearts and minds
Using all their senses
Breathe in the life you might be missing
See the world as children do
Walk in wonder

A Feather's Life

The wind and clouds were home for some time
Until I floated downward
On a sweater I did lay
Where I nestled myself in, so warm and safe
Upon a bench I stayed
Hearing children play along the way
This would be my home; so I thought that day

As a hand almost picked me up
A light breeze fluttered my feathery spirit
Taking flight once again
Circling in the air
I spun in a spiral motion
Till a bird flew away with me
We traveled so long
Losing all sense of direction
He must have enjoyed me tickling his beak
This would be home; so I thought that day

With a bird call he let me go
Neighboring with the wind and clouds by my side
My ride was coming to a close
I braced myself for the worst
But so softly I drifted
Until my heart lifted
As I realized I fell into a nest
On a branch my home to rest

A Postcard

Remembering the postcard taped to my wall
I couldn't believe I was here
Walking the infamous roads of Amsterdam
I was captivated by the church bells

Every hour the bells would chime
Resonating through the narrow streets
As I looked up, I saw ladder-shaped rooftops
An endless staircase of triangulated hills

The buildings were all linked together
Creating mazes with every changing road
Following the streets always led to an opening
Where bridges crossed the landscape

Mom's hand in mine, my feet dragged
Slowing down my pace, but not excitement
Reaching the top, I gazed at the bridges one after the other
The dikes filled with boats on either side

Water-ways surrounding these small towns with bridges
Unmovable, fixed in place
I could feel the rich history of this land
It all began with a postcard

Time Stealers

Time stealers
Lurking in dark places
Making you miss those memorable days
Those ordinary whatever days
That escape so easily from our grasp
The yesterdays you'll never earn back

Trying to find the time lost is an endless battle
Memories of the could-have-beens
Disappear from the family album
Flipping through, you only see the blank pages
Desperately you try to move the hands of time
But those are do-overs you will never find

Hold on to your ordinary whatever days
Time will only be of regret
If you grab the somethings
From the time stealers
Hold the someones in your life
The passionate things you do
You will end up having gained time
Through the moments you have found

Sowing the Garden

As I walk through the unknowns of life
The uncertainties of what a day brings
The unpleasantries that sting
You, oh Lord, are cradling me in Your arms
Holding me with care and unmeasurable strength

In everything I face You aren't surprised
You laid out my plan without compromise
At times I want to break free
When I don't have the eyes to see
But I remember in all situations
Your love prevails undoubtedly

The vision You have for me to grow
How to get there or where I should go
Is like a garden to sow
For flowers abloom
Leaves room for joy to flourish
For hearts to nourish
If God's hand uses His tender fingers
To enrich the earth
How much more are we worth
With that realization
My hands are outstretched for You to hold
You are the woodcarver
I am the mold

On bended knee I will praise Thee
Glory be to the One who made me

I Noticed

The intricate details of life
Escape our eyes
Fleeting to oneself
Till the magical beauty of a pond
Utterly captivating
Reveals a mystery
Beauty of a hummingbird
A rarity few see
But there you are
In front of me
Drinking water from a flower bloom
Perfection of flight
Delicately placed feathers
The vibrancy of colors, of truest form
Are brought to my eyes
Navigating a flower trail, I watch
You are a vision
Indescribable
Unmeasurable
Mesmerizing moments
I'll take with me
Knowing I was in the details
Of a hummingbird's life

The Wills of Fear

Capabilities are not hindered
Possibilities remain uncovered
Even though physical hardships you endure
This does not slow you
In any shape or form
Richness of your life
Remains full

Others with no physical hindrances
Go through the motions of life
Stopping their goals and aspirations
Finding frozen opportunities by their feet
Their comings and goings are of hardship
Creating pause
Moments fleeting

Fear itself is clear
To paralyze days
The years away
Your heart
Covered with this emotion
Binds you
Holding your life in stillness

Landscape of beauty
Flowers of color
Trees following the breeze
Fear never touches these
In thunder nor wind
Snow or sleet
Beauty remains

Open your eyes, then you will see
A life to live so free
Fear
When coming toward you
Guard your heart from this taking hold
See the richness of life

Let your reflection
See your bright colors
Opportunities are in your hand
Searching the footprints of the land
The journeys you will go
Only in time will you know
The endless splendor
When you walk in the fields of life

The Diamonds of the Lake

The boats move into the harbor
The setting sun draws them in
Its pathway brilliantly shines on the sails
Leaving sparkling diamonds trailing behind
Hidden treasures the lake keeps for her own
The jewels dance
Under the royal blue sky
Never taken from people's hands

Until the darkness hugs the earth
The jewels are no more
Disappearing
Sinking
On the lake's sandy floor
In the evenings after
The sun
Opens up her treasure chest
Of jewels and diamonds
Glistening for the sails to enjoy
Floating
On the cool waters

The Silent Lullaby

Softness as of a turtledove's wing
Silently singing in the garden
I cradle you in my arms
A joyous glow radiates from your face
In the presence of angels
Eyes now heavy in slumber
They close to rest
A peacefulness lays upon my breast
A tenderness shared
While rocking you in our chair
The angelic sweet lullabies
To your ears they bring
For you to hear them sing

The Bridge Between Two Nations

Kneeling before my love
On this bridge between two nations
Reminds me of the bridge
Connecting us
An American and Canadian
My eyes look into your heart
With excitement and anticipation
Because my love stands before me
Eyes blue as the sky
A face like an angel
I have found my one true love
The one to share a life together
As a lover and friend now and forever

– Emil Ureel
To my one true love, the poet, Sara Ureel

Ripples of Love

A leap of faith
That's what love is
No book or map can prepare us so
For the days ahead
Where we might go
Love is not happiness felt all the time
Storms will come
The waves will form
The ripples of love will be tested
Like a sailboat finding the wind to move
So is love when finding a clearing
During the storms together we battle
Sometimes love can drift away
A commitment is for always
Our love remains the anchor
That pulls us back into shore
You bring me to your arms
Love grabs hold of us once more

Perfect Imperfections

Putting my "face" on in the morning
Looking my best
You give me the eyes I seek
The kiss I anticipate

But when I'm plain
With my "comfys" on
I unexpectedly see those same eyes
A kiss, never anticipated
You smile at me
Making me blush with my "cutesy" ways

Rewinding back to college life
The same happened then
The spark is still there
My fairy tale, I still have

Unspoken

Your hand in mine
We are the lovebirds
Sitting on the dock

With our toes touching ever so slightly
We feel the cool water lap at our feet
As the ripples move to the shoreline

Moonbeams shimmer the lake like glass
Fragments of light touch our interlocking hands
Like glistening diamonds

Your hand in mine
We are the lovebirds
Sitting on the dock

No words are shared
Only our unspoken I love you's
Are heard

Countless Years of Lasting Love

Growing up I saw your love
Radiate in our home
When I saw you laugh in each other's arms
Tears sometimes flowed down your cheeks
Jokes and humor
Only the two of you would find amusing

Secretly loving
Those unexpected surprises
You both had your secret love languages
Only a couple knows where they began
Those are the days to remember
The tender moments
Never forgotten

The sun did go behind the clouds
Allowing the pouring rains to fall
Everything would be upside down
The delicate strings of marriage remained strong
Rooted to grow

Those struggles were blessings in disguise
The hurts were forgiven and forgotten
The bonds strengthened
The hardships you overcame
Those are the days to remember

Your love always came through
Few seem to find
But after countless years
You have one of those stories
Of happily ever afters

Shades of Love

Beautiful shades of love
My wedding gown took your breath away
Walking down the aisle was our first day
Of our future as one, we couldn't be happier

Starting a family of five our house got busier
Tag-teaming of who goes where and when
Family outings and special dinners
Never were missed

Our children grew
Like all of them do
Slipping through our fingers
They too found loves of their own

But the shades of love
Like sands in an hourglass
Shifted when your accident happened
Calls circled the phone lines

The man I married was lost to a brain hemorrhage
I grieved
A different you
I was walking down the aisle to

Our future as one continues to be
Your teachings of wisdom will remain strong in our family
The role model you were
We are striving to become

More weight was put on my shoulders
Switching hats from caregiver to around-the-clock nurse
The beautiful shades of love evident
I carry through my days; you remain my beloved

Like endless wildflowers in a field of grass
Like dew holding onto the flower petals
So will I always have
Your constant love

Your eyes still light up
Whenever I walk by
A true testimony
What true love is

Never-ending
Never ceasing
Beautiful
Shades of love

Your Hands

Cuts, bruises with blackened fingernails
Your baby girl would slip her tiny hands in yours
Like a cave, my hand would get lost
I would admire their roughness
The mazes of grooves and lines
The textures of scars that followed
Stories to go with each one
Your outdoor adventures in gardens
The long hours from sunrise to sunset
I believed you were invincible
With surpassing strength
As decades pass
It's as sweet now
Slipping my hands in yours
A rush of memories engraved in my mind
Of your strength and love so evident and remaining
Telling their own stories
Of how they came to be and who you are now
The hands I admire and love
Waiting for the next time I can slip my hands in yours

A Mother's Heart

A mama bird
Wraps her young under her wings
Feathers keeping them warm as she sings
On alert she is always
Ready to swoop in

Mothers have the same heart
Holding their little ones with such care
Until their hurts are no longer there
Soothing their tears; they disappear
Ready to swoop in

The comfort of a mother's embrace
A soft touch felt on their hands, their face
Makes my little ones feel so safe
Years seem to fly
When a mom is watching by their side

You don't need me swooping in
In doing so
I'd hurt you I know
Your independence is given
When you do your own livin'

Knowledge is earned when situations arise
When you find out how to stand firm
How to compromise
My sweet children you will always be
Flying now solo, independently

Precious Little One

As you took your first breath
I cradled you in my arms
As my tears fell on your cheek
I gazed into your eyes

A beautiful baby — so perfect
You were our blessing from above

We loved all the firsts you gave us
A smile, a stretch
Cooing as babies do
If I only knew these firsts would be few

I would have held you longer
Kissed you sweeter

A blessing God gave us
Now has been taken
Years pass and an emptiness can be still felt within
Unanswered questions haunt me
An ache that never leaves
A hole never filled

We should not question
God's divine perfection
You needed my special little one
A heavenly purpose, unknown to me

For my little one, with eyes so kind
A face so soft
A heart so full of love
Is in Your kingdom with angels

Even though our moments were fleeting
The times we shared were precious

You were a blessing from God
To us
To the angels
To the heavenly realms
Till I see you again, my precious little one
In our heavenly home

The Legacy You Leave Behind

Three little words
So precious for us to hear
Sometimes fell on deaf ears
I sought
For all the things
You could not do or speak
Your ten little fingers and toes I caressed
Our love never wavered
Moment by moment was savored
Your crippled hands and feet
You were almost motionless, voiceless

What a valued life you had
Giving the world a true perspective
When the light in your eyes shone
You brought sunlight to another person's day
When your smile bounced off your face
It landed on mine
When your laughter filled the room
Tears would stop from falling
You were the perfect reflection
Of what we all strive to be but cannot achieve
You fully embodied what beauty is

In the simplest ways
You taught us how to be selfless
The importance of kindness
By letting us come into your world
With a touch of your hand
A soft embrace
A short conversation
A kiss upon your face
A tender moment indescribable
Unexpected gifts you gave

For all the things you could not do or speak
You did in ways I never thought possible
Those three little words, I heard you say
I love you too

Before Me – Guiding My Path

Your nurturing spirit
Made me feel loved undoubtedly
Even on the worst of days
Love remained
Hope seen around the corner

Your giving heart and helpful hands
Taught me to take the time to do the extras
Because the smallest acts of kindness
Can mean more than you know to another

You showed me your enjoyment
Being in the details of my life
You taught me the value of being a mother
Opening my eyes to the wonderment of motherhood

During those childhood years you gave me a gift
That I began to see
When I cradled my own children in my arms
Rediscovering the sweetness I saw you have

Glimmers of you, shimmer in my life as a reflection
I see the beauty of motherhood in which you delighted
You were woven through my life's journey as a child
The treasures you so willingly gave, I embrace with my own

The Unmovable Rock

Dew hugs the grass tips
Mist hovers over the parks
The sun's bold colors
Slowly touch everything in its wake
Breathing in the morning air
I notice

In this moment I am reminded
Of God's goodness
His faithfulness and promises
Nature, reeling us in
Again and again
Tugging at our hearts
Drawing us closer to Him

When ugliness looms its head
I immerse myself in God's beauty
He surpasses all
In that knowledge I stand strong
He is my Rock
That will not be shaken

A Stroll to Nowhere

Rooted in the rich soil
Bouquets of garden flowers blossom
Fragrant honeysuckles
Entice fleeting hummingbirds to drink their nectar
The whispering wind
Brings sweet sounds to nature's ear
Hills come alive with their song
Birds fly over majestic trees
Whistling to the land in harmony
To the water's edge
I stroll with a smile
Simplicity at its core
Takes hold of my heart
Touching my soul
Glorious gifts from God to unwrap daily

Where the Wind Blows

Life brings love and joy
Pain and suffering
Everything God places in our path has purpose
Sometimes we have to let the wind blow
Where it goes
No one knows
Trust in Him, who put us there
He intricately made us with care
His loving hands are always ready
To make the waves steady

A Step Forward

When we are children
We receive the most praise
From saying a simple coo or phrase
When we stumble or fall
Arms pick us up
It doesn't matter the mess-ups we make
Only the efforts we take
The times we fail are celebrated

As we become adults
The praises are few and far between
Failures are recognized
There is no reassurance or drive
Our dreams, slipping through our fingers
Disappear in the wind
With that our desire to reach the impossible
Is buried

You saw failures as opportunities to redesign
I'm inspired by your iron will
To carry on climbing the steep hill
Running beyond the discouraging words
Looking over the horizon few find
Running the race toward your dreams

Kaleidoscope of Love

Time
How it once was
In our kiss
A soft embrace
Your hand in mine
Love remains
Washing over me
All over again

Like a kaleidoscope
That you view through
Becomes a dream
As you turn the dial
Patterns
Colors move
Ever-changing
Beauty remaining

The years pass
Like sand in an hourglass
Looking into each other's eyes
You see what is
Forever and will be
True love
Beautiful and timeless

Hope Transformed

It Found Me Again Today

My imaginary safety nets
I like to keep near
To control everything I hold dear
But it found me again today
Change
With no warning it came

Throughout my comings and goings
Change is what makes me shy away
Keeping me at bay
My life has been folded up like a map
Stored away from any light of day
I put myself there

Where do the roads lead
If undriven, I will never know
Where will quests take me
If unopened, I will never follow
Where are the uncharted waters
If I don't look, I won't search for them

To pursue anything
We need to jump with a leap of faith
I am ready to take the wheel
To steer into the unknowns
To open the map of uncertainties
Of change

The Author of My Story

A sense of shame
Is attached to flaws and darkness
A life – undesirable

If I were the author of my story
Nothing would resemble my life
Tweaking and altering
Stories of pains and hurts
I would erase
Losing those memories
I never wanted

Flaws and darkness can bring about courage and strength
Sculpting our life
Self-awareness heightened when redefined
I wouldn't know
The circumstances that brought us together
The unpleasantries I needed to have happen
The significance of losing love
When I thought forever was painted on the walls
The subsequent events started the chain reaction
Watching the compass change course
To the desired destination

Trust in the story given to you
A valued purpose we have
Embrace with outstretched arms

Our Author knows the words that need to be written
The pages that need to turn
With tangled knots
Twisting and turning
Surrounding us are the murky waters
Sometimes falling is a necessity
To see the clarity through the eye of the storm

We should move forward in any posture
You are by our side
Navigating with Your hand
Out of the whirling winds
We battle
To find our lives You have written
One with details
You are the Author of our story
You should never be erased

Jaded Reflections

Jaded reflections
Looking back at me
Mirroring everything I don't want to see
Why can't I be
Someone
Unlike me

Jaded reflections
Twist my world of realities
Chokehold my dreams and aspirations
Where everything sacred and pure
Becomes broken off with shattered glass fragments
Scattered everywhere I walk

The shards of glass blanket the morning dew
Outline my life's journey
Piercing my walk with every new step
Dusk settles in, I lay my head down to find peace
But only torment and echoes of poisonous words
Ring through my mind

The stains and scars of my life haven't escaped me
When the sun awakens me
Slipping further away, I find myself in a place of despair
None of the bandages I tried to mend matter
Spiraling down the rabbit hole
Only emptiness and loneliness envelop me
A darkness I finally succumb to

Hope – sometimes invisible to the naked eye
Will always find you
Never was I lost
My Shepherd was looking for me
His hands of pure Light hold my whole being
Wrapping me in satin,
He takes me out of the bondage I was enslaved in
The stains of my life, Jesus took upon himself
Taking on the hell of my realities
Removing the tarnish of my ways
Now I am washed
Whiter than snow
A mirror of God's likeness is my reflection

My aspirations have become inspirational
My dreams unbounded
Unraveling into possibilities
The jaded reflection renewed
My fragmented life restored
I see the someone in my reflection
The me – I'm destined to be

Breaking Free

My wings were cut off
My dreams snuffed out
I could not soar in the skies above
My will was not my own
Trapped in a life unwanted

But then You came along
Loving the person I am
The doubts diminishing from my mind
The invisible ropes tied around my wrists
Were loosened
Broken

I learned how to mute the voices from all sides
Capable possibilities magnify
Limitless journeys
Doorways opening
The world at my fingertips
A new pair of wings
To soar again

Cookie Cutters

Cookie cutters of design
Nothing unique individually
All line up in rows
Ready to march in step

We live playing follow the leader
Attitudes and beliefs
Designing and shaping us
Don't question or challenge
What's acceptable
Permissible
Our views become skewed

Our †rue identity
Is from our Creator's hand
Designing with precision our individuality
The Heavens above answer the questions below
Our unique design
Following the Leader of Truth

Finding Our Perspective

Gazing up at the multitude of stars
How insignificant are we
A streak of light shoots across the moon
How uninspiring are we
Freshly watered flowers
Move ever so slightly in the sun
How ordinary are we

As I walked down the road
A child was helping their grandma into a car
How significant can we be
I saw a teacher breathe hope
In a room of students with despair
How unknowingly inspiring are we
When you hug me with such devotion
How can ordinary be nothing less than extraordinary

Life is full of possibilities
Dreams ready to be found
Open the door to a new day
Be significant in someone else's life
Be inspiring in countless ways
Be ordinary
Which is extraordinary
Change our world in small insignificant ways
We all hold significant value

Seasons

During the crashing waves
The passing tides
I fell into your arms of love
At times we sank to the ocean floor
Hitting rock bottom
We remained anchored
Slowly moving up to the surface
We got caught in the undertow
Grabbing hold of us
Pulling us down
To the hardships and struggles that collide
In the pulling and turbulence of waves
We learned how to swim
When life put us in a tailspin
Making us stronger as we battled through

In times we flew to the light of the clouds
To the moonbeams of night
Watching the shooting stars of life
Breathing in the comfort of our love
With beauty around us
Flying as one
Having the revelation
That true love exists in the world

Life has seasons
We all go through
Ones to keep
And the ones we want to breeze through
The richness comes however
During those dark places we travel
When our life is tested

Embrace with open arms
The challenges we are given
When the walls are closing in
Opportunities of growth
Around the corner await
These will bring us to a new dawn
If we sail there together
With our hands ready
For the seasons of life

Through a Camera Lens

The lens remains unfocused
The flash untouched
The pictures are nevermore
For the emptiness and brokenness of her days
Filled her heart with loss

Try once more
Holding the camera in your hand
See the missed pictures that capture hope
The love that resides down the side streets of town
Laughter is heard from children
Standing beside the buildings of the city
The birdsongs
Echo under the bridges

We live in a fragmented world
A stained glass of cut pieces
We cannot stay in the brokenness of life
These can be fused together
Reflecting a beautiful light
Array of color
Where healing happens
Love continues
Where hope lives on

A Missing Puzzle Piece

A single missed puzzle piece
Never found
A painting blotted out
Never recognizable

We all have an urge
To critique ourselves
Our capabilities
Attainable possibilities
Weakness
Our missing puzzle pieces
Our blurred vision
Of who we really are

Unlike landscapes, taken over by the land
We visit and hold dear
Weeds that create foliage
Wildflowers that bloom
Pond reeds that loom
Into the curvatures
Of the water's surface

Trees that fan the breeze
Grass lush under our feet
We hold the frame
Beauty in our eyes
The flaws and corrections
We blindly miss
Admiring
Breathing in the peacefulness

In the same likeness
So should we
Love our whole self internally
With the missing puzzle piece in hand
Release them from the land
Into the sky to disappear
Only then will it be clear
The beauty within us we should all hold dear

Open the Windows of Heaven

As I slipped my hand in yours
I prayed for moments more
But you were ready for your wings
For where the angels sing
Where peace resides
Where perfect love rests

I'm not left behind
Looking upon the timeless stars
My eyes became transfixed
To the brilliance that exists
Stars are the windows to heaven's door
The moonbeams from its corridor
With a breeze from your wings
Touching my hair
The whispering winds
That brought them there
I'm lost in a memory of my own

Your presence is made known
As I admire your heavenly home

The Air I Breathe

In my waiting
I take a destination to nowhere
On mountainous terrain
You call my name
You're alongside me
Walking in step
Whispering in my ear
Your quiet demeanor
I find my rest there

Walking in the hills
The rugged climb
Ferns' caress
The bristling leaves quiver
Branches sway
Looking up Your way
With every brush of nature
Your presence is made known

Deeper into nowhere
Birds sing their lullabies
Echoing in the valleys
Water streams over the moss-covered rocks
Crossing over the brook
I find reflections of You everywhere
In my waiting
A somewhat stagnant home
A peace settles in my soul
My faith is grown
Spiritual hunger is fed
You are closer than the air I breathe
Thy living water
Flowing through me

Inch by Inch

A caterpillar inching up a stem
A bird in the freezing rain
Waiting for a worm to pop out again
We all endure the uphill battle of days
In different ways we climb
Continuing the journey of time
We run
On empty
Tired
The mountains we are on
The troublesome days that give way
We all have to bear

Don't grow weary
God will carry
The load
On our backs
The weight
On our shoulders

Continuing forward in the battles we face
Moving inch by inch with grace
With determination
We grow
In lengths
That only God knows

The Artist

Without the Artist's vision
Our perspective is murky
Realities are misunderstood
Inspiration misplaced
The unknowns are prevalent

The Artist sees the world through a different lens
He's all-knowing
Truth is there for the taking
If we follow Him
Thereby opening our eyes anew

When we cultivate His land
The grounds display beauty
That lay there once before
The hands of our Artist
Molded it into being

Colors that spring up
Serenity in nature
Resemble the Artist's palette
Capturing the fluidity
A life with Christ

The insignificant beauty we can miss
Like the tranquility of nature's kiss
Submerge yourself in His word
Unshakeable joy given
When we become His paintbrush
For the Artist to use

Wings

As the wings take to the sky
The image I had of our world
The strength I thought we held
Reversed
Transformed
For the wings in the air showed me
Life in the skies above
As the earth drew further away
Clouds were the trees of green
The sky mirrored the grass from below
Opening my mind to the universe
Its wonderments and complexities
The mysteries it holds
That no one can truly see
We are given a glimpse of the heavenly realms
The Milky Way of stars
The galaxies beyond
These lie above our understanding
Until God touches our eyes and opens our minds
Take the time to share the glimpses of our awaited eternity

Whiter than Snow

When walls are closing in
When in the light of day
Darkness remains
Anxiety finds its home
Despair settles in

With a whisper, hum, or thought
Like a gentle breeze touching your arm
Feel Jesus
On the doorstep of your heart
Waiting to be let in

He breaks down the closing walls
Overwhelming despair, a distant memory
Evil lurking in the shadows
His light buries and shines eternal

He moves mountains
Without lifting a finger
Out of the deepest valley
He carries you
He changes the hardest of hearts
Into the whitest of snow

The Snowflake

The drifting snow
Gently falls upon my face
The noise of the world fades
In the flurries of the night sky
A peace settles on the ground
I am alone
With You
Your heavenly hand touches me
With every snowflake
You are felt
The white softness You leave behind
I walk through

Like a warm blanket
You wrap me in
To hold
Placing a memory of a story
Long foretold
I gaze up to the heavens
One star shines so bright
Oh, what a sight
In the darkest of night

The shepherds followed the same light
To a babe in a manger
In swaddling cloth You lay
To live with us beginning that day
You come to me this very night
Reminding me of the starry light
The shepherds and angels that appeared
To see the King
Which the season of celebration brings
In the simplest form you came
Your story comes to me this year
In a snowflake
Drifting

Anxiety Freeze

When fear sets in
Anxiety and worry start to penetrate through
Freezing what is
I mentally stop the hands on the clock
But at that moment
Your voice is heard
Reminding me of my purpose
Revealing to me in time
Your ways, oh Lord, are divine
Even amongst the ugliness and pain
I shall find rest
Let my heart always beat to Your rhythm
For each moment of every day
Faith in You will open my eyes
To the beautiful carvings in my life
A work of art
Your hands created

On the Ready

I will always be on the ready
In my heart
In my dreams
To put my faith in You
I feel Your arms around me
Knowing I never walk alone
You tear down the walls I build
When I'm spiraling down in life's abyss
I call upon Your name to feel
Your outstretched arms
Holding me like a child
Your reign over the land
You know the number of each grain of sand
When I am lacking in my faith
You are on the ready
To move in my life.

Nature's Tune
In My Life

For All Our Tomorrows

As the moon disappears in the night sky
With clouds in its path
I'm at peace
Knowing the moon's light will shine in the tomorrows

As I drive my morning commute, I see the sun's rays
Peeking over the horizon
I breathe in a smile of awe
Looking forward to tomorrow's wonderment in the sky

As I gaze into the twinkling stars
I marvel at the countless sparkles
Encompassing the darkness
Ready for tomorrow's performance

The faith we seem to have in the creation of the unknowns
The belief we hold true
That the wonders of our world will meet us again
How much more faith do we need
That God put everything in its rightful place
For the tomorrows of our days

Strokes of Color

The paintbrush strokes the canvas
Color slowly emerges
The white easel transforms
Into shapes and curvatures only the artist recognizes

His Hand moved on our earth's canvas
Color bursting in all directions
The nothingness became something of beauty
That in an instant surpasses all artists

Staring at a still life on a wall
I admire the artist's hand
Making the decisions of what paint to use
To bring life to the painting

Walking through a trail with a canopy of trees
I wonder if we can admire
Our Artist of Life
Who created the reality of the still life paintings of the world
Whose paintbrush is never put down

The Unknown Orchestra

In my hammock, I lay as the orchestra plays
The wind sweeps through and it begins

The trees slowly dance
Side by side they sway

The cherry blossoms take flight
Like wind instruments they rustle through my hair

The branches bend in step
While the leaves whisper their sounds in unison

My cares
A distant memory
As the orchestra plays on

The Fisherman

Staring out into the horizon
The fisherman sets sail
Where the water ends
Where the horizon begins
It's seamless
A mystery

Only a fisherman would search
Where the horizon meets the sea
Becoming one with nature
The sights are overtaken by beauty
His eyes mystified

The fisherman's figure fades
As the morning mist waves in
Making the scene a mystical glow
Fanning the rays of light
Onto the water's surface

The fish outsmarted him today
But the fisherman knows
His journey goes beyond the fishing line and hook
It's about sharing the untold stories

As the sail anchors the shoreline
The exploration of the day has ended
The water still calling the fisherman

Nature's Deep Sleep

The night sky
Brought the flower to bloom
From the stillness of the evening air
Darkness touched the soft petals
The lightning bugs illuminated the leaves of green
That fly in the quiet skies above

The cooling soil is welcomed
From the hot summer sun that was
The fragrance of the flower takes to the air
Where the morning dew
Lies on the freshly opened petals
With hymns
The birds awaken nature's deep sleep

Where the sun warms the earth
Yellows and reds deepen
As the sun rises
Having the privilege to see
The flower that bloomed
Under the night sky

The Midnight Sun

The moon brilliantly shines
Wildflowers delight
Under the shimmering night
As we sleep the flowers glisten
The midnight sun
Reveals and listens
To the tapestry of stars
The enchanting glimmers of light
Touching
The earth's surface

In the wake of a fragrant field
Deer scamper
The cooling soil is felt
By the crawlers of the ground
Hugging the roots of plants and trees
Mazing through their hidden tunnels
The echoing valley
Hears the owl call
Like church bells the owl awakens
The creatures of the nightfall

The Golden Pathways

In the wheat fields
Wildflowers touched the land
Playing peek-a-boo with the wind
The rhythm of the breeze
Made the wildflowers sway
As I walked the untouched lands of gold
I created pathways with my footsteps
But only for a moment
As I saw the grass spring back behind me
Like I was a memory
From another time
I lay my head
On nature's soft bed
With my body resting
On the earth's grass
Letting only time pass
Smelling the sweet fragrance
The wildflowers showed their brilliance
I touched their delicate petals with my fingertips
The red, yellow, and white blooms
Filled my eyes
Warmed my heart
Calmed my spirit
Understanding that beauty can only be valued
If one takes to the disappearing pathways
Of the wheat fields

Supporting Hands

So tall they stand
Rugged in place
With their peeling bark upon their face
With their outstretched arms they lend a hand
To the plants beside
The gift of shade is given

Sighs of relief are heard
While the limp leaves of flowers perk up
They find rest under the branches
Of the birch trees

To show their musical talent
A breath of air rolls in
Moving the forgotten grasses like waves of water
Rustling leaves are brought to a chatter
The flowers dance to the rhythm of the breeze
The radiant sun stands high
Above the sky of blue
The last performance of color
Lands on the birch trees' rugged bark
Glowing a fiery red
With leaves resembling flames
As the sun sets behind the birch trees

Renewal

The pouring rain
Brings billowing clouds of gray
Pushing away colors from above
Dreariness sets in
Awaken your eyes
See the flowers moving with each fallen drop
Watch as colors deepen
Lifting tired petals
Quenching the earth
A lush setting moves in
Lowering the curtain of dreariness to the ground
To fallen rains
Ushering new life

The Arduous Climb

I am waiting
For Your timing
To move my mountain
Prayers are effortless but seem hopeless
Without a cause
Your timing is heavy to bear
Where are You to listen

I am anguished
When I see pebbles tumbling past
For my prayers were for an immediate blast
To move the mountainous terrain
I seek You for refuge
I call upon Your Name
For strength I do not have
You are the Rock standing steadfast
Though I am stumbling
My world is crumbling

The arduous climb of branches and snares
Is everywhere I follow
I fall to the ground and wallow in shame
My hope is diminished
I am lost and in pain

You help lift my head from the dirt—
I rise to my feet
Now with strides
My mountain appears to be a hillside
In awe, with the view I left behind
The journey I climbed

Looking at the sights below
Never did the mountain change
Perplexed I thought
Mountains are as pebbles on the ground
That the Almighty can kick around
For reasons unknown
That may never be shown
The mountain was for me to endure
Until a day without warning came
The mountain disappeared

You moved it in Your time
You kicked the stones by Your feet
The mountain was my defeat
Only through my humbleness and reliance
Was it possible
When I focused on You
Much was learned in turn
With me in Your favor
I'm grounded
Knowing You are my Saviour

Life's Refining Waves

Reflections of light
Shimmer in the fading night
Diamonds glisten
As the rippling water
Moves and listens
To the cool winds pushing against the lake
Even stillness
Brings a tune below where the current follows

Our life moves similarly
A rippling effect
Continually shaping our story
That touches each part of our journey

A life of ease creates a hole of emptiness
Never filled
The storms and billowing waves
Are where life is made

About the Author

As children raised in the Netherlands during World War II, Dirk Romkema and Aukje Muller immigrated to Canada for a new beginning. There they married and raised my two older siblings and me. As a young girl, I remember watching my father paint landscapes on canvas, which beautifully reflected his profession as a landscaper. I see parallels in my own life as I capture the natural beauty that surrounds me with paper and pen.

From camping trips to beach outings, I loved swimming far into the lake and diving under the waves as they approached. Feeling the power over my head, back, and toes, I marveled at the reflections of the setting sun. My childhood connection with nature brings meaning to my book Life Reflections, a composite of poetry, which captures memorable moments and the rippling waves that life brings.

After graduating from Humber College with a degree in early childhood education, I continued my studies at Calvin College. It was there that I met Emil, my college sweetheart, who remains the love of my life. We married in June of 2000 and have raised our three children in Holland, Michigan.

Inspiration from the Lord and Emil's encouragement deepened my own enthusiasm for writing, which blossomed in the summer of 2021. I felt like a flower blooming in the springtime, finding my hidden love, like a rosebud waiting to fan out into something of beauty. My pen has become an invisible paintbrush bringing inspiration to life.